21ˢᵗ
Century
Skills Library

GLOBAL PRODUCTS

CELL PHONES

Kevin Cunningham

Cherry Lake Publishing
Ann Arbor, Michigan

Published in the United States of America by Cherry Lake Publishing
Ann Arbor, MI
www.cherrylakepublishing.com

Content Adviser: Edward Kolodziej, PhD, Director, Global Studies Program,
University of Illinois, Champaign, Illinois

Photo Credits: Cover and page 1, © Jim Craigmyle/Corbis; page 4, Photo courtesy of the
Library of Congress; page 13, © Reuters/Corbis; page 19, Photo courtesy of Alexander
Needham; page 21, © TWPhoto/Corbis; page 25, © Michael S. Yamashita/Corbis

Map by XNR Productions Inc.

*Cherry Lake Publishing would like to acknowledge the work of
The Partnership for 21st Century Skills.
Please visit www.21stcenturyskills.org for more information.*

TABLE OF CONTENTS

CHAPTER ONE

GETTING THE MESSAGE

In the 1800s, people sent messages over long distances by telegraph.

Rex, his older sister Bonnie, and their father Dan were eating dinner when the cell phone clipped on Dan's belt rang. "Hello?" he answered. Rex and Bonnie looked at each other as Dan listened and then spoke for a few seconds. As he folded the phone shut, he stood up.

"Who was that?" Rex asked.

"One of my employees," Dan said. "He's having some trouble. I have to go back to work."

Bonnie frowned. "He's not supposed to call during dinner."

"It's not dinnertime where he is," Dan said. "Right now, he's in Australia."

"I didn't know cell phones reached that far," Rex said.

"You can call anywhere in the world with them," Dan said as he emptied his plate. "I couldn't have the business I have without being able to reach people in China, India, France—all over the world. Before cell phones, it was a lot harder to communicate with people in other countries."

"How did people do it?" Bonnie asked.

"By putting messages in bottles," Rex said.

"Not exactly," Dan said, and then he offered them a quick explanation of how people started communicating with one another.

"Starting in the 1860s, people sent written messages by code through **telegraph** cables that ships had laid on the bottom of the Atlantic Ocean. In 1902, the ship *Silvertown* laid the first section of another cable from Ocean Beach in San Francisco to Honolulu, Hawaii. It began operating on January 1, 1903. Later that year, cables were laid from Honolulu to the Midway Islands, then from Midway to Guam, and then from Guam to Manila in the Philippines—clear across the Pacific Ocean. When I was born, back in the 1960s, people still sent important messages to other countries that way.

By then, telephone calls could cross the ocean through copper wires inside cables at the bottom of the sea. But that was still a new way of doing things.

"In the late 1980s, phone calls traveled through high-tech glass fibers— inside cables, like before. You could hear the calls better, and it became cheaper to make a call across the ocean. Today, if you are using a special satellite phone, the phone sends signals to a satellite in orbit around Earth,

Portable radio-phones were used by the military during World War II.

and the satellite sends it to the phone you're calling. Regular cell phones, on the other hand, **uplink** and **downlink** through the cellular network, not directly through a phone-satellite-phone connection."

∾

The ideas that led to cell phones go back to the 1920s when police departments sent messages to squad cars over special radios. Then during World War II, the military used portable radio-phones to communicate on battlefields.

Two companies in particular searched for ways to make telephones mobile. American Telephone and Telegraph (AT&T), then the largest communications company in the world, invented the car phone, the first mobile phone to be widely used. The car phone needed an automobile's electrical power and an antenna to work. It could not be carried around, though a few companies adapted early car phones into portable (and heavy) "briefcase phones" for a short time.

Meanwhile, executives at Motorola spent millions of dollars to create a handheld phone that was easier to carry around. In 1973, a Motorola engineer named Martin Cooper took a **prototype** of the new invention to New York City. It weighed almost 2 pounds (0.9 kilograms) and was 10 inches (25.4 centimeters) long and 3 inches (7.6 cm) thick. On April 3, Cooper stood on a busy street corner and called a rival researcher at

21st Century Content

Cell phones are used around the world. Nokia, a corporation based in Espoo, Finland (near Helsinki), leads the way. Today, about one out of every three cell phone models sold is a Nokia. Other leading companies include Motorola of Schaumburg, Illinois, and Sagem Communication, a corporation in Paris, France.

These companies and many others have improved the cell phone. Today's models weigh only a few ounces. You can buy one of the less-expensive models for less than $100, much less than the cost of a cell phone twenty or even ten years ago.

Why do you think the cost of a cell phone has decreased over the years?

Bell Labs. His bulky prototype started the cellular telephone revolution.

The first cellular phone system in the United States was launched in 1983 in Chicago. By then, engineers had made the cell phone a little smaller. It weighed 1 pound (0.45 kg), half as much as the prototype. Over the next ten years, cities and towns across the country gave permission for companies to build cellular systems. By 1995, twenty-five million Americans owned cell phones.

The cell phone has changed the global economy in huge ways. It allows people, like Rex and Bonnie's dad, to easily keep in contact with their workers, partners, and clients, even when traveling in a remote country. The global economy, in turn, has made it possible to build cell phones and sell them at low prices. The different **components**, or parts of the phone, come from countries thousands of miles apart.

CHAPTER TWO

TANTALUM

After Dan went back to work, Rex and Bonnie eagerly ran to the computer to search for information about cell phones. The conversation with their dad at dinner had sparked their interest!

"I still don't get it. How does that little phone manage to reach people in Australia?" Rex asked.

Bonnie typed away at the keyboard, looking for answers to Rex's question.

"Ah, here's something!" said Bonnie. "On this Web site, they talk about what cell phones are made out of."

Bonnie and Rex read on to find out more about how cell phones are manufactured and produced.

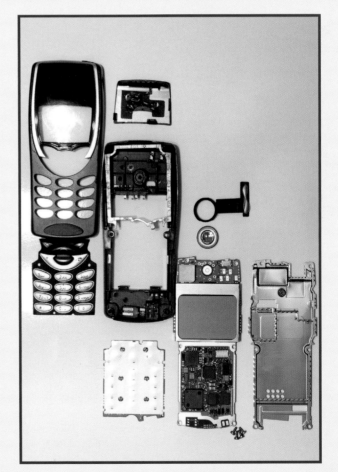

A cell phone is made of many different components.

One of the most important components of the cell phone is a rare metal called tantalum. This blue-gray metal is very hard and very rare. Most of the tantalum used in cellular phones comes from Australia, Brazil, and Canada.

Australia produces the most tantalum. Mines operated by a single company, Sons of Gwalia, Ltd., provide more than half of the tantalum used today. Australian mines draw most of their tantalum from a quartz-heavy rock called pegmatite, and pegmatite sources provide the majority of the world's tantalum.

Cassiterite, an **ore** associated with tin, yields tantalum, too. For years, mines extracted tin from cassiterite and discarded the leftover rock—a material miners call slag. No one guessed that the traces of tantalum in the slag would one day be valuable.

Tantalum is also found in coltan, an ore made up of columbite (col-) and tantalite (-tan). The tantalite contains the tantalum.

Major producers in Australia, Brazil, and Canada often take tantalum from two or more sources. Other possible sources, including a rare kind of granite, are also being investigated.

The tantalum at the Sons of Gwalia sites in Australia is taken from open pits dug out by heavy equipment and explosives. The rock then undergoes refining. Acids are applied to the raw ore to make it dissolve

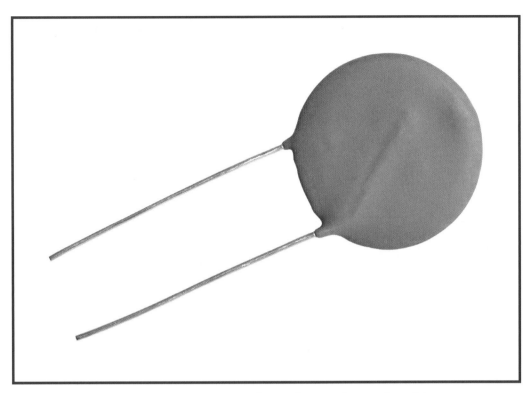

Tantalum is one component used to make capacitors such as this one.

into a watery slop called a slurry. As the slurry goes through special filters, each element is separated from the others.

Once the tantalum is refined, it is sent to manufacturers that specialize in turning it into forms used in products. Two companies dominate this part of the tantalum industry: Cabot Corporation and H. C. Starck.

Both Cabot and Starck turn tantalum into a variety of products. But when it comes to cellular phones, the most important product is tantalum powder. Approximately 60 percent of it goes to make one of the cell phone's most important components—the capacitor.

THE COLTAN RUSH

The Democratic Republic of Congo (DRC), a central African nation, has huge reserves of tantalum. The DRC's tantalum comes primarily from coltan.

In the late 1990s, the DRC's coltan briefly became an important part of the cell phone industry. At the time, consumers in the United States, Europe, and East Asia were eager to buy cell phones, laptop computers, and video game systems. Companies needed tantalum to build—and sell—more products.

One of the laws of economics is the law of supply and demand. According to the law of supply and demand, the price of a good—like tantalum—will go up if it becomes hard to find (supply) or if more people or companies want what's available (demand).

Demand for the world's tantalum drove up the price. Africans hoping to escape poverty or get rich flocked to the eastern Democratic Republic of Congo to mine coltan. The DRC is one of the world's poorest nations. At the time, the average worker only made $10 per month. A coltan miner, on the other hand, made $10 to $50 every week.

There was a high cost, however. Violent clashes between rival army groups over the best mining areas killed thousands of civilians. Miners also caused severe environmental damage by gouging out holes in the rain forests. Hungry workers even slaughtered the region's rare eastern lowland gorillas for food.

Companies in other parts of the world, upset by the conditions, refused to buy coltan mined in the DRC. The lack of demand caused the price of DRC coltan to fall. By 2002, the rush was over.

The violence in the DRC forced many people to leave their homes.

CHAPTER THREE

CELL PHONE COMPONENTS

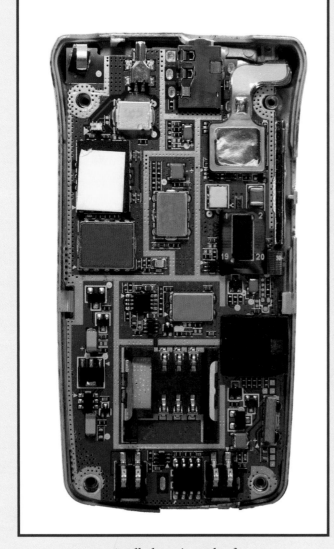

A cell phone is made of many small parts.

"Ah, so cell phones are made out of tantalum," Rex concluded.

"No, the cell phone's **capacitor** is made out of tantalum," Bonnie said.

"But what is the capacitor, and how does it work to get Dad's voice all the way to Australia like a regular phone?" Rex questioned.

"I'm not sure," Bonnie said quizzically. Puzzled, and searching for answers, Bonnie and Rex continued looking for information.

"We know what the capacitor is made out of, but what other parts are there in the cell phone?" asked Rex.

"Let's search the phrase 'cell phone parts' and see what we come up with," Bonnie suggested.

Bonnie and Rex entered the search terms, opening up a wealth of information on the components of the cell phone and how they work to make the cell phone function properly.

The capacitor is a vital part of a cellular phone. Put simply, it stores and moves electricity through the device at a reliable rate. Capacitor manufacturers like tantalum powder because electricity passes through it exceptionally well. Tantalum capacitors are considered efficient—even a small capacitor can do a lot of work.

Engineers have, in recent years, invented a number of smaller capacitors. This has helped manufacturers develop smaller cell phones with more features. These tiny capacitors also go into

Learning & Innovation Skills

Communication technology has evolved at a rapid pace since the 1800s. What changes in technology do you think are likely in the next few years? What impact do you think these changes will have on your life?

other products such as medical implants like insulin pumps. Small capacitors even shape the electronics used in aircraft and spacecraft.

As important as it is, the capacitor is only one part of a cell phone. In fact, cellular phones are impressively complicated considering their small size.

A cell phone draws its power from a battery. Usually it uses a lithium-ion battery, a type that can be recharged and one that can be manufactured in various sizes to fit inside different products. As many users of cell phones and laptop computers know, however, lithium-ion batteries wear out, even when not in use, and they are sensitive—even dangerous—when exposed to heat. Japan-based Sony Corporation pioneered lithium-ion batteries in electronics devices and remains one of their largest manufacturers.

Battery factories can be found in many countries, but a number of them dot the southern Chinese city of Shenzhen, a center for high-tech products of many kinds. Having so many components made in China helps cell phone companies build each finished phone at a low price.

The cell phone's screen depends on a liquid crystal display, or LCD. The light LCD comes from fluorescent lights that are slightly thinner than a pencil. The light shines through a filter and eventually a layer of liquid crystal, a substance that has some qualities that make it behave like a liquid and others that make it behave like a solid. In its natural state, liquid crystal appears twisted. Passing electric current through it causes the liquid crystal to change its structure.

Untwisted liquid crystal keeps light from passing through a filter at the opposite end. The part of the display where there is untwisted liquid crystal becomes darker. That is why the information that appears on the LCD screen when we call up a phone number or other information appears darker than the rest of the screen.

As with many electronics, LCDs are manufactured in China, with Shenzhen and the surrounding area a leading center. Taipei and South Korea also have substantial electronics industries.

There are, of course, numerous other components to a cell phone, such as microchips, the speaker to hear through, the microphone to speak through, and even the plastic that houses the device.

CHAPTER FOUR

Putting the Parts Together

"Wow! I never knew that there were so many tiny parts in such a small phone." exclaimed Rex.

"But how do they manage to get cell phones to people all over the world?" asked Bonnie.

Both Bonnie and Rex looked at each other, amazed at all of the things they were finding out about the cell phone. But they still wanted to know just how such a small little gadget gets people to speak and listen to one another from different parts of the world.

Rex took over at the computer as they searched deeper into their online resources to figure out how cell phones managed to get into millions of people's hands all over the world.

Business is booming in Taijin, China. Commuters clog the superhighways at rush hour. Rich company executives and poor factory workers have little in common. But members of both groups carry cell phones.

In China, the cell phone is a symbol. Carrying one means you work hard and that you are serious about getting ahead in China's growing economy. More than 250 million Chinese use cell phones. Even though that number represents only part of China's population, it's close to the total number of people in the United States—300 million people.

Many businesses have offices and factories in Taijin, China.

A number of cell phone manufacturers have plants in Taijin or in nearby areas. In recent years, workers have flooded in from the countryside for jobs. It is tedious work. Partially manufactured phones pass by on a conveyor belt. It is the worker's job to fit the same piece to each phone, hour after hour. Far more women than men fill the **workforce**. They make $70 a month. The roles played by men and women in Chinese society are different than those accepted today in Western cultures. One difference is that men are almost always in charge of the workers.

Finished phones bound for overseas are hauled by the thousands in containers via trucks or trains. Their destinations are bustling port cities such as Shanghai, Shenzhen, and Hong Kong.

A typical container is 8 feet (2.4 meter) wide and just over 8 feet (2.4 m) tall. A container is

Workers assemble cell phones in a factory.

either 20 (6.1 m) or 40 feet (12.2 m) long. Containers are **standardized**,

or made the same sizes, for a reason. Matching containers can be stacked

and pushed close to one another—which uses all the space efficiently and allows the maximum number of containers to be stored. With standardized containers, every port in the world can handle the cargo in the most efficient way possible. Moving massive amounts of product quickly and reliably is essential if companies want to make a profit. And that profit is essential to fuel world trade.

In the shipping industry, a single 20-foot (6.1-m) container is called a twenty-foot equivalent unit, or TEU. (A 40-foot (12.2-m) container equals two TEUs.) Shippers measure a load in TEUs. The supership *Emma Maersk* officially can carry 11,000 TEUs and may be able to cram on an additional 3,000 TEUs. Ports also use the TEU as a way to measure the amount of product that passes through. In 2005, Singapore claimed to be the world's busiest container handler after moving more than 23 million TEUs.

Dockworkers load these thousands of containers onto containerships, the workhorse vehicles of the global economy.

CHAPTER FIVE

THE GLOBAL ECONOMY

Containers of goods are loaded onto a cargo ship for other markets.

"So, Rex," Bonnie went on to explain, "containerships are the way companies and factories manage to get their products from one place to another."

"Ah, I think I get it! So if a cell phone factory in Hong Kong wants people in San Francisco to have cell phones, they just load them onto containerships and send them overseas," said Rex.

The *Emma Maersk*, a super-containership, is truly enormous. If stood on its end, the 1,302-foot (397-m) vessel would be the world's seventh-tallest building. At about 184 feet (56 m) wide, it cannot fit through the Panama Canal. The canal's locks, the massive machinery that lifts ships between the canal's various sections, can only handle ships up to 110 feet (33.5 m) wide. The government of Panama plans to widen the famous canal so that containerships such as the *Emma Maersk*, and even bigger vessels yet to be built, can pass through. How do you think these large ships will continue to change the way goods are produced and shipped in the future?

"Exactly!" Bonnie concluded. "You've got it."

"So it's no wonder Dad was able to talk to his worker in Australia. Perhaps the cell phones they were using to talk to one another were made in one of those factories we read about and brought to them by containership."

It is hard to imagine today's global economy without containerships. Almost eight thousand of these massive vehicles sail the world's oceans. The megaships haul thousands of containers in their **holds**. More containers are piled on the deck.

Containerships only need a small crew. Typically, about twenty sailors plus a few officers serve on the vessel. A sailor earns about $1,000 per month caring for machinery, cleaning and painting, and keeping a late-night watch from the ship's bridge. Though hardly a fortune, the pay is often much better than the jobs offered in the sailor's home country.

A containership voyage is usually uneventful, but the crew still needs to watch for threats. Storms on

A group of pirates travels by speedboat on the South China Sea.

the open sea can generate waves big enough to carry containers right off the deck. On occasion, massive, unexpected waves have sent entire ships to the bottom of the ocean. The busy routes used by containerships also draw pirates. The pirates zip out on quick speedboats and board a ship. Often they steal what they can before vanishing into the dark. Other times, they take over the ship and hurt or kill crew members.

A containership can cross the Pacific Ocean in about two weeks, depending on weather, how many stops it makes on the way, and other factors. When the ship reaches its destination, workers rush out to greet it. Cranes swing into place and begin to unload the containers. Each

Containerships allow companies to move products from one place to another at a low price. For example, a television manufacturer in China can ship its product as far as Great Britain for about $10 per TV.

Low cost is one of the reasons cellular phone companies build telephones in faraway places like China when they intend to sell the product in the United States. Companies can pay a worker $70 a month in China, far less than they would have to pay a U.S. worker. Building phones there saves money, even when the cost of shipping is included.

container has a list of its contents. The cellular phones and other products inside will be sent on to future customers.

Often whole containers are moved by truck or freight train to storage facilities owned by the parent company, to wholesalers (who sell the product at a profit to their own customers), or to large warehouses owned by large electronics stores. Each of these warehouses serves a specific geographic area. Workers there send out shipments of cell phones to individual stores as the stores demand them.

The cellular phone reflects the reach of the global economy. It's possible that the tantalum used in a phone began its journey in the hands of miners in Australia, Brazil, or Canada. Along the way, it became powder in factories in Germany or the United States and was used to make capacitors in high-tech facilities in Great Britain. The phone itself, the end product, may have been built by the hands of a young Chinese woman.

Just as the cell phone can reach the entire world, it is a product from the entire world.

❧

When Dan arrived home from his office visit, Rex and Bonnie couldn't wait to share their new knowledge.

"Dad, Bonnie and I learned what cell phone capacitors are made from—tantalum!" Rex proclaimed.

"We also learned that people everywhere can use cell phones because containerships carry cell phones from factories where they are made to places all over the world."

"Sounds like you both have been doing a little online research. I'm impressed!" Dan said encouragingly, amazed by his kids' enthusiasm.

"So Dad, can Rex and I have cell phones?" Bonnie asked shyly. Dan laughed a little bit and said, "Maybe when you are a little older! Cell phones are not toys and you need to prove that you will take care of a phone and use it properly. But knowing how they are made, what they do, and how they work are good first steps. You're starting to convince me that soon you'll be ready to be a responsible cell phone user."

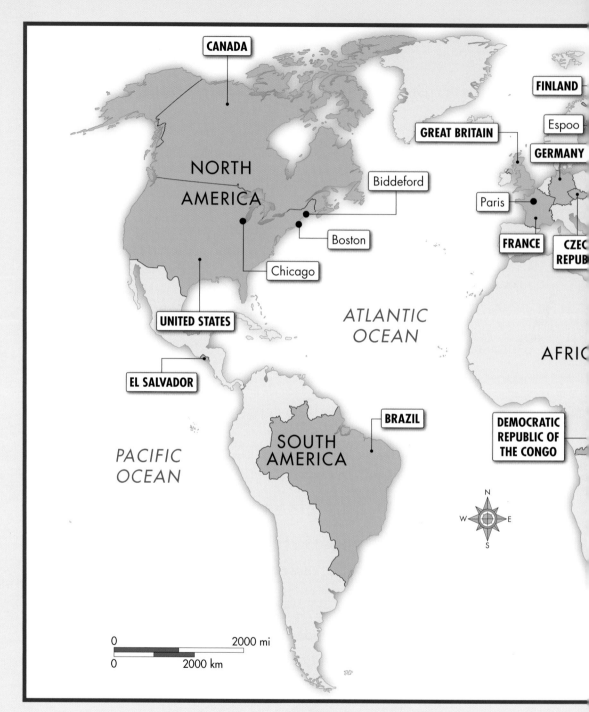

This map shows the countries and cities mentioned in the text.

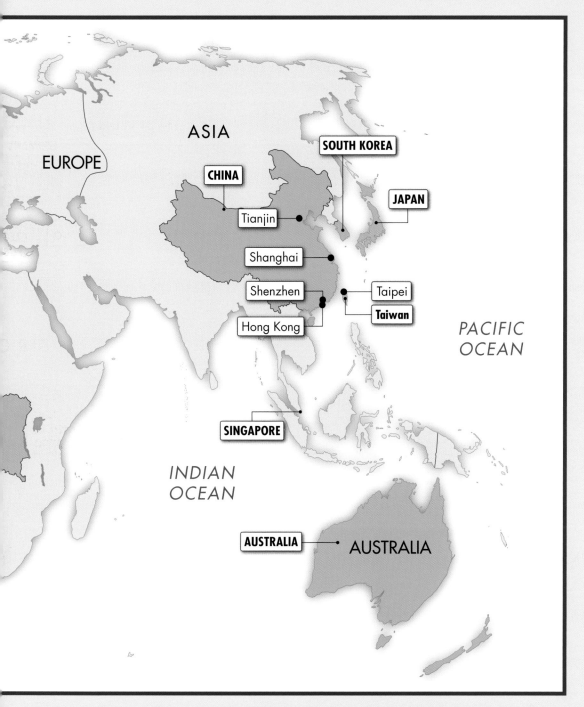

ASIA

EUROPE

SOUTH KOREA

CHINA

JAPAN

Tianjin

Shanghai

Shenzhen

Taipei

Taiwan

Hong Kong

PACIFIC
OCEAN

INDIAN
OCEAN

SINGAPORE

AUSTRALIA

AUSTRALIA

They are the locations of some of the companies involved in the making and selling of cell phones.

Glossary

capacitor (kuh-PA-sih-tur) A capacitor is a device that stores electricity and moves it through a device at a reliable rate.

components (kuhm-POH-nuhnts) Components are specific pieces of a device.

consumers (kuhn-SOO-murz) Consumers are people who buy and use goods and services.

downlink (DOUN-lingk) To downlink is to transmit data from a spacecraft or satellite to a receiver on Earth.

holds (HOHLDS) Holds are the cargo storage areas of ships.

ore (OR) Ore is the raw mineral material that contains a specific kind of substance, such as tantalum or gold, that is mixed in with other kinds of rock.

prototype (PRO-tuh-tipe) A prototype is a working model of a new invention.

reserves (ri-ZURVZ) Reserves are the amount of a mineral resource that has been discovered but hasn't been taken from the ground.

standardized (STAN-dur-dized) If a product is standardized, then each one made is exactly the same.

telegraph (TEL-uh-graf) A device that allows messages to be sent by coded electrical signals over wire or radio.

uplink (UP-lingk) To uplink is to transmit data from a facility on Earth to a spacecraft or satellite.

workforce (WURK-forss) A workforce is the number of workers in a specific workplace or industry. It can also mean all the available workers in a state, country, or other geographic area.

FOR MORE INFORMATION

Books

Dramer, Kim. *People's Republic of China.* Danbury, CT: Children's Press, 2006.

McPhee, John. *Uncommon Carriers.* New York: Farrar, Straus, and Giroux, 2006.

Willis, Terri. *Democratic Republic of the Congo.* Danbury, CT: Children's Press, 2004.

Web Sites

Federal Communications Commission: History of Cell Phones
www.fcc.gov/kidszone/history_cellphone.html
For a brief history of the cell phone

Los Alamos National Laboratory: Tantalum
http://periodic.lanl.gov/elements/73.html
For more information about tantalum

INDEX

ABOUT THE AUTHOR

Kevin Cunningham is the author of several books,
including biographies of Joseph Stalin and J. Edgar
Hoover and a series on diseases in human history.
He lives in Chicago.